Twas the Night of First Christmas!

**Story, Online Musical Audio Book
and Family Gathering Guide**

Written & Illustrated by Jamie Kearney

Rhythm & Music by Chris Kearney

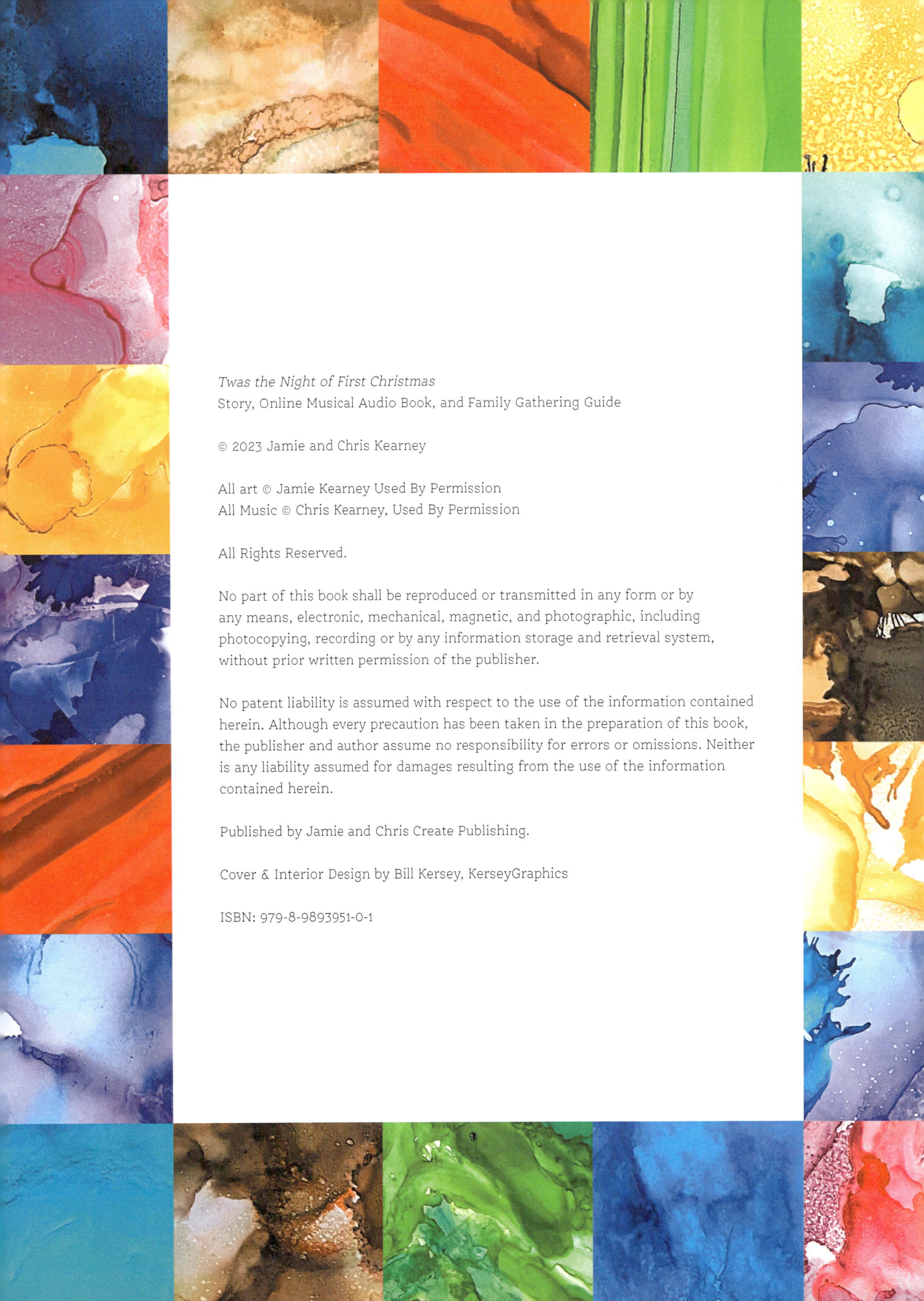

Twas the Night of First Christmas
Story, Online Musical Audio Book, and Family Gathering Guide

© 2023 Jamie and Chris Kearney

All art © Jamie Kearney Used By Permission
All Music © Chris Kearney, Used By Permission

All Rights Reserved.

No part of this book shall be reproduced or transmitted in any form or by any means, electronic, mechanical, magnetic, and photographic, including photocopying, recording or by any information storage and retrieval system, without prior written permission of the publisher.

No patent liability is assumed with respect to the use of the information contained herein. Although every precaution has been taken in the preparation of this book, the publisher and author assume no responsibility for errors or omissions. Neither is any liability assumed for damages resulting from the use of the information contained herein.

Published by Jamie and Chris Create Publishing.

Cover & Interior Design by Bill Kersey, KerseyGraphics

ISBN: 979-8-9893951-0-1

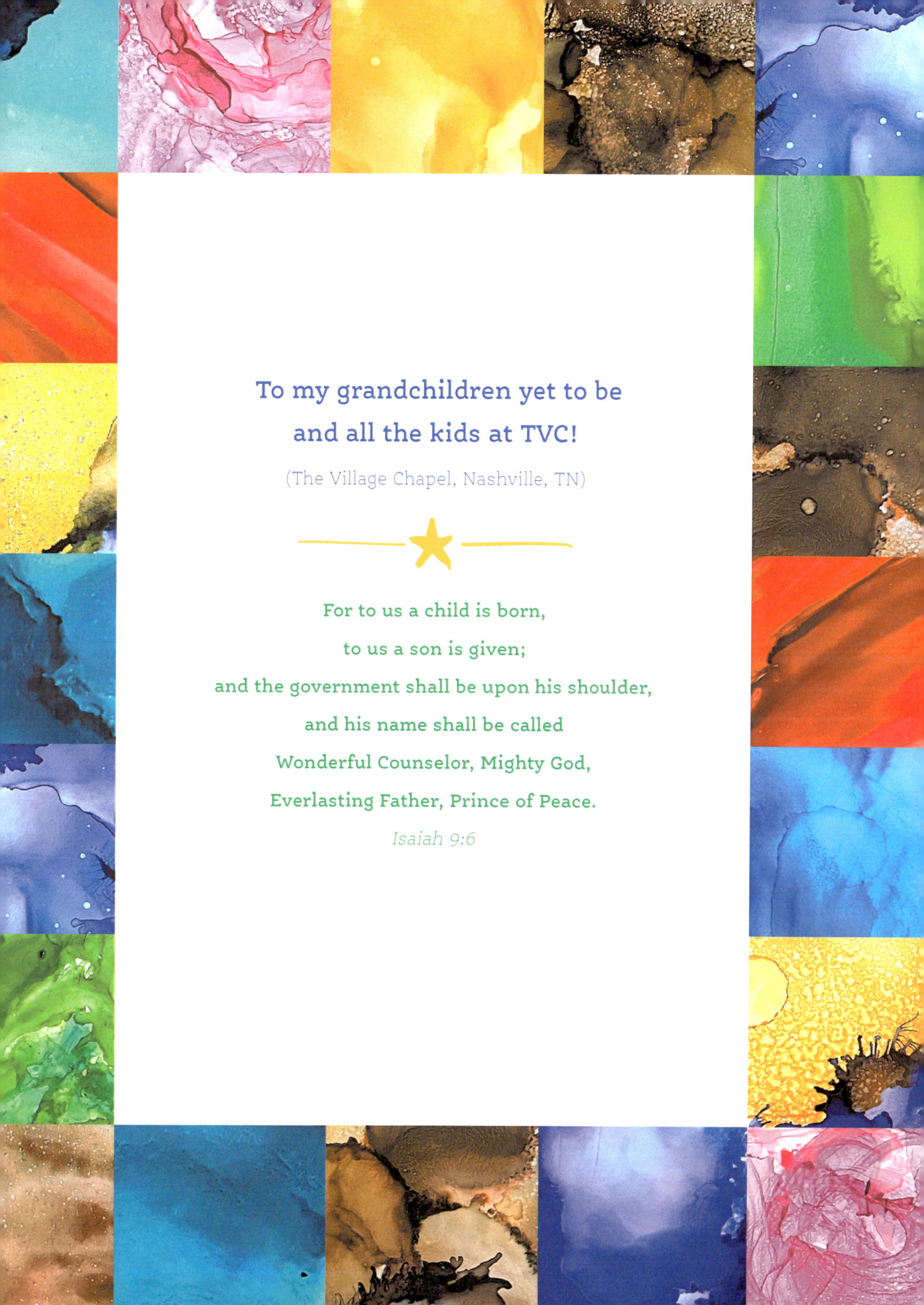

**To my grandchildren yet to be
and all the kids at TVC!**

(The Village Chapel, Nashville, TN)

For to us a child is born,
to us a son is given;
and the government shall be upon his shoulder,
and his name shall be called
Wonderful Counselor, Mighty God,
Everlasting Father, Prince of Peace.

Isaiah 9:6

As you read this story of a new baby king,

I hope you will find a place to stop and sing.

Follow this code to hear this read aloud book,

now open the pages & take a look!

https://jamieandchriscreate.com/christmasbook

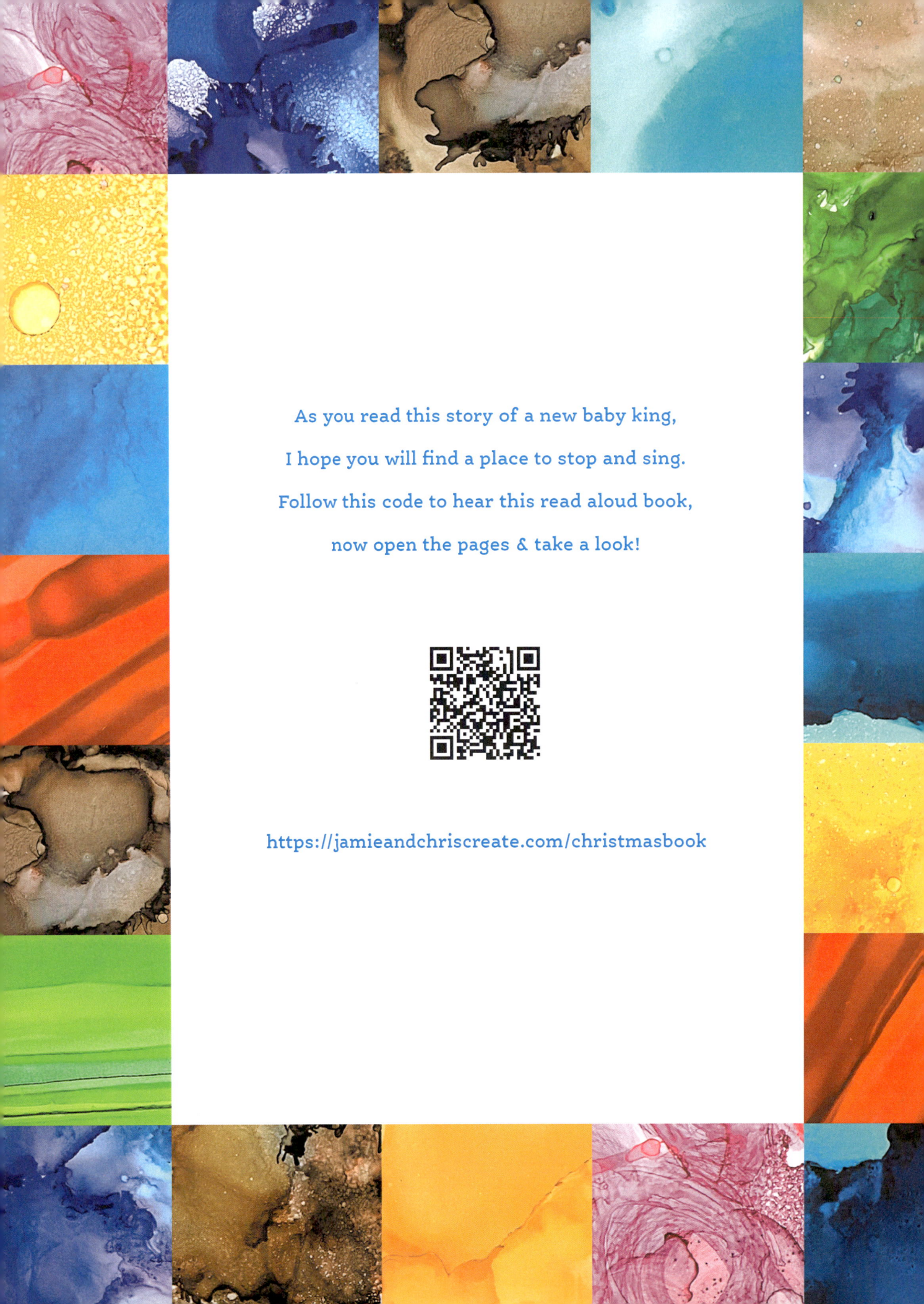

Voiced by:

Intro: Jamie Kearney

Gabriel: Isaiah Kearney

Mary: Lylah Nash

Joseph: Chris Kearney

Shepherd: Kevin Tucker

Wise Man #1: Pastor Jim Thomas

Wise Man #2: Pastor Matt Pierson

Wiseman #3: Pastor Tommy Bailey

Star: Isabella Kearney

He Shines: Jamie Kearney

Key, Drums, Percussion & Fun Sounds: Chris Kearney

First Christmas

Twas the night of first Christmas
and all through the house,
Every creature was stirring,
yes, even the mouse
The star was hung high
over the stable with care
while shepherds & kings said,
"Hey, look over there!"
For under the star was the true baby king
and all of God's angels that night came to sing!

The Angel Gabriel

"Silent night, Holy night all is calm all is….."

Oh Hi, I am the Angel Gabriel

I heard you were coming to hear my story from the stable.

My home in heaven has much to tell

But none makes us sing like the story of the baby king.

It all started way back when

God appointed me messenger to men.

I was surprised & didn't know what this job would hold

but off I went, just as I was told

to tell the great story about to enfold.

First God sent me to Mary,

I got to tell her about the baby she would carry…

Mary

I am Mary, pretty ordinary,

I worship God & help my mom.

Until the day Gabriel came

with news of my baby to be,

not so ordinarily

"Do not be afraid" he said,

but all I wanted was to hide my head

Still I listened, & heard of God's favor,

as I stood in fear & wonder

why He chose ordinary me,

to mother His extraordinary baby

Joseph

I am Joseph the great great great great great

grandson of David the King

Remember David? He was the King

who loved to praise and sing!

We had heard a Savior would come from his family line

But I never thought this would be God's chosen time.

Gabriel told me not to worry while in a dream

I was given the honor of being on Gods team!

So off to Bethlehem we went Mary, the baby and me

Oh the place we would go and the wonder I would see

There was no room at the inn so in a manger He lay

Baby Jesus was born on this first Christmas day!

The Shepherd

It's dark and I'm lonely out with my sheep in the cold
About the life of a Shepherd, there's not much to be told
Except on this magnificent night,
the sky was filled with heaven's light
God's Angel arrived he was so strong and so bright
I must admit, I was afraid of the sight
But the Angel said, "I bring you good news of great joy
Go to Bethlehem to meet God's baby boy!"
Then the skies opened wide and angels we found
singing Glory to God, what a wonderful sound!
As quick as they came the angels flew from the sky
and I thought to myself, I wonder why,
God sent angels to me, a shepherd with sheep
my heart was so full I just could not sleep
So I ran to the stable & fell to my knees
I worshiped the king & He seemed pleased.

The Wise Men

We are the wise men numbered one two & three

and we traveled from a land too faraway to see

we followed the star because that's what we do

and found baby Jesus, coo

but we never expected animals who moo.

Some call us wise & some call us kings

but most of the time, all you hear about are the things

that we brought to the child, so precious and new

He is the king, this much is true

but to us He is more and we vowed to protect,

the birth of God's son when Herod would object

so we left on a path no one else knew

and would no longer spy for Herod who

would bring end, to the life of our new baby friend

The Star

Lights! Camera! Action!

Oh this job brings me such satisfaction!

Now children you know that each night I shine bright,

but never so bright as that cold winter night.

As I made my entrance on stage for my show,

God had a plan that I didn't know

My costume that day shone brighter than most,

as if the director wanted me to host,

a night of friends, some big and some small,

waiting for them to come one and come all!

So they followed my light, through all the dark night,

till gathered together we bowed at the sight

And I smiled at a light brighter than mine

It was sweet Baby Jesus who forever will shine!

He Shines

✝

He shines for the wise men

whose bows are so deep

and even for shepherds

so lonely with sheep.

He shines for young Mary & girls just like you

& Joseph and men who hearts are kept true.

He shines for the hurting, the lost,

and the weak

He shines for all who are willing to seek

His love and his mercy so strong and so true,

Whether your weeping or leaping,

He's there for you.

He shines for all those willing to say

Merry Christmas in this special way.

Family time, heart to heart questions for clever kids of every age!

Questions for younger kids

- When was the first Christmas?
- Who put the star over the stable?
- What do we call the star over the stable?
- Who is the true Baby King?
- Why do you think God chose Mary to be Jesus mom?
- Joseph was in the family line of David. Can you name some relatives in your family line?
- Why did Joseph and Mary have to travel to Bethlehem?
- What was life like to be a Shepherd?
- Why do you think God sent the Angels to visit the Shepherds?
- Do you know any other people in the Bible who were Shepherds? Hint: Joseph's great, great, great, great, great grandfather.
- What did the Angels tell the Shepherds?

- How did the Wise Men travel to Bethlehem?
- How did they find Jesus?
- What gifts did the Wise Men bring to Jesus?
- What gift would you give to Jesus?
- The Star of Bethlehem shone brighter than all the stars, why?
- Who made Star shine so bright?
- Jesus, the Light of the World shines brighter than any star or person ever. He wants all of us to turn and follow Him.
- Who does He shine for?
- How can you shine to lead people to Jesus? (don't worry if you need help with this one, just turn the pages for some fun ideas)

Questions for older kids

- What is the true meaning of Christmas? Who & why are we celebrating?
- What are some of the Angels' jobs?
- Who lives in Heaven?
- What was the message Gabriel brought to Mary?
- What was the message Gabriel brought to Joseph?
- Mary was young, and had no children, why do you think God chose her to be Jesus' mom? When God looks at you, what are the qualities He sees in you?
- How did we know Jesus would come from the family line of David?
- What does the name Bethlehem mean?
- David was the king of who?
- Why was there no room at the inn in Bethlehem?
- The job of a Shepherd may seem unimportant, but God chose to send His Angels to them. Why do you think He chose them? What other people in the Bible were Shepherds before they did big things for God and His people?

- What was the message the Angels brought to the Shepherds? Where can you find it in the Bible?
- Where did the Wise Men travel from, and how did they find the stable?
- Why do you think they chose the gifts they brought to Jesus?
- What gift would you give to Jesus?
- Who was Herod and why did he not like Jesus?
- There are people today that do not like Jesus, why do you think that is?
- The Star of Bethlehem lead people to Jesus. How can you shine the light of the Lord to lead people to Him.
- Jesus, the Light of the World, shines to draw all to turn to Him. Is there anyone He would not shine for?

**Have you ever told a friend about Jesus?
I hope you will use this fun Christmas story to help share who Jesus is and how He loves you!**

Let's put this story into ACTION!

So, now that you know the true story of Baby Jesus and all that He means to us, what can we do to celebrate His story? Jesus is the Greatest Gift ever given to our world! I know you want to share that gift with your friends and family?

You are creative kids who are so full of faith. One great way to grow in your faith is to tell others the stories of the Bible. From before the beginning of time God knew he would send His son, Jesus to earth. God sent Him and He came because He loves us so very much!

I hope you will tell your friends, and to give you a little help along the way, here is an easy way to share. Yes, you can read this book to them but after that you can do more. You can live this story out loud, putting what we have learned from each character into ACTION!

Here are 7 action words that go with the 7 characters from this story

Love like Jesus

Proclaim like the Angels

Listen like Mary

Abide like Joseph

Believe like the Shepherds

Give like the Wise Men

Shine like the Star

Love
like Jesus

Jesus replied, "Love the Lord your God with all your heart and with all your soul. Love Him with all your mind.' This is the first and most important commandment. And the second is like it. 'Love your neighbor as you love yourself'.

Mark 12: 30-31

There is no greater love than the love Jesus has for you. He left heaven and came to earth to be born in a stable. He grew and taught His disciples so that we could learn to be disciples. Finally, He gave His life on a cross to pay for our sins. We can never repay Him but we can obey Him. This is one way Jesus taught us to love.

How can you love your neighbor?

- Spend time with someone you love playing the game they chose.
- Write a card or letter and send it to a friend.
- Surprise your mom and clean your room before she asks.
- Read John 3:16 with your family & thank Jesus for coming to earth for us!
- Draw a picture of a heart & write the names of people you love in it. Thank God for these people.
- Draw a picture of a heart & write the names of people who love you in it. Thank God for these people.

Proclaim
like the Angel

Sing to the Lord; praise His name. Each day proclaim the good news that He saves!

Psalm 96:2-4

One of the top jobs of an angel is to Proclaim! Proclaim means to let everyone know, to announce, or send a message... and in the case of Angels they are proclaiming the best news from God! What did they tell the Shepherds?

How can you Proclaim the news of Jesus this Christmas?

How can you proclaim?

- Read Luke 2:8-14 with your family. Practice it, memorize it, so you can share the story with friends.
- Go caroling with family & friends. Sing the songs that celebrate Jesus coming.
- Draw a picture of the angels who came to the shepherds in the fields. What did they say?
- Wish everyone you see this week a Merry Christmas or Happy Holidays.
- Make a card for each member of your family. Proclaim, or say something kind about them & remember to tell them Jesus loves them.

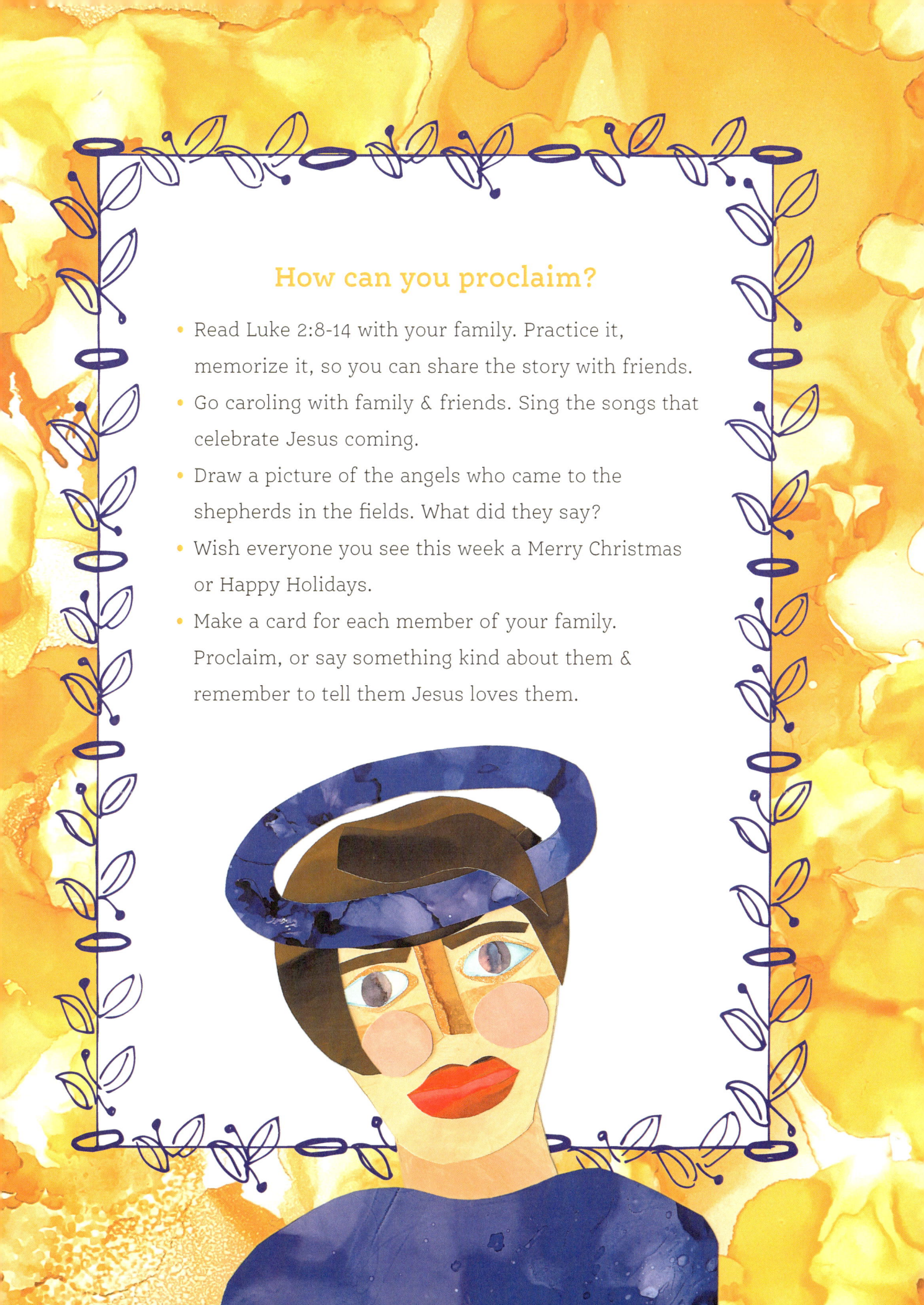

Listen
Like Mary

Therefore everyone who hears these words of mine and puts them into practice is like a wise man who built his house on the rock

Matthew 7:24

Mary was young, just a teenager, & yet God was asking her to become the mother of Jesus! She could have rebelled like kids, teenagers, & even adults do sometimes but instead she quietly listened to the Angel Gabriel as he proclaimed the Word of God's plan for her. Do you listen, to God's word? Are you ready to obey Him when He asks you to do hard things?

How can you listen for God?

- Listen to a worship song with your family & thank God for sending Jesus
  Reflect upon the things that the Holy Spirit brings.
- Go with your family on a walk & stay silent. Listen to God's Creation.
- Practice a moment of silence, draw a picture of what you hear in your heart.
- Ask your parents or grandparents to tell you how they first met the Lord. Were they kids or adults, was it at church or through a friend? Sit quietly & listen, thank God for the older people in your life who know Jesus & will share Him with you.

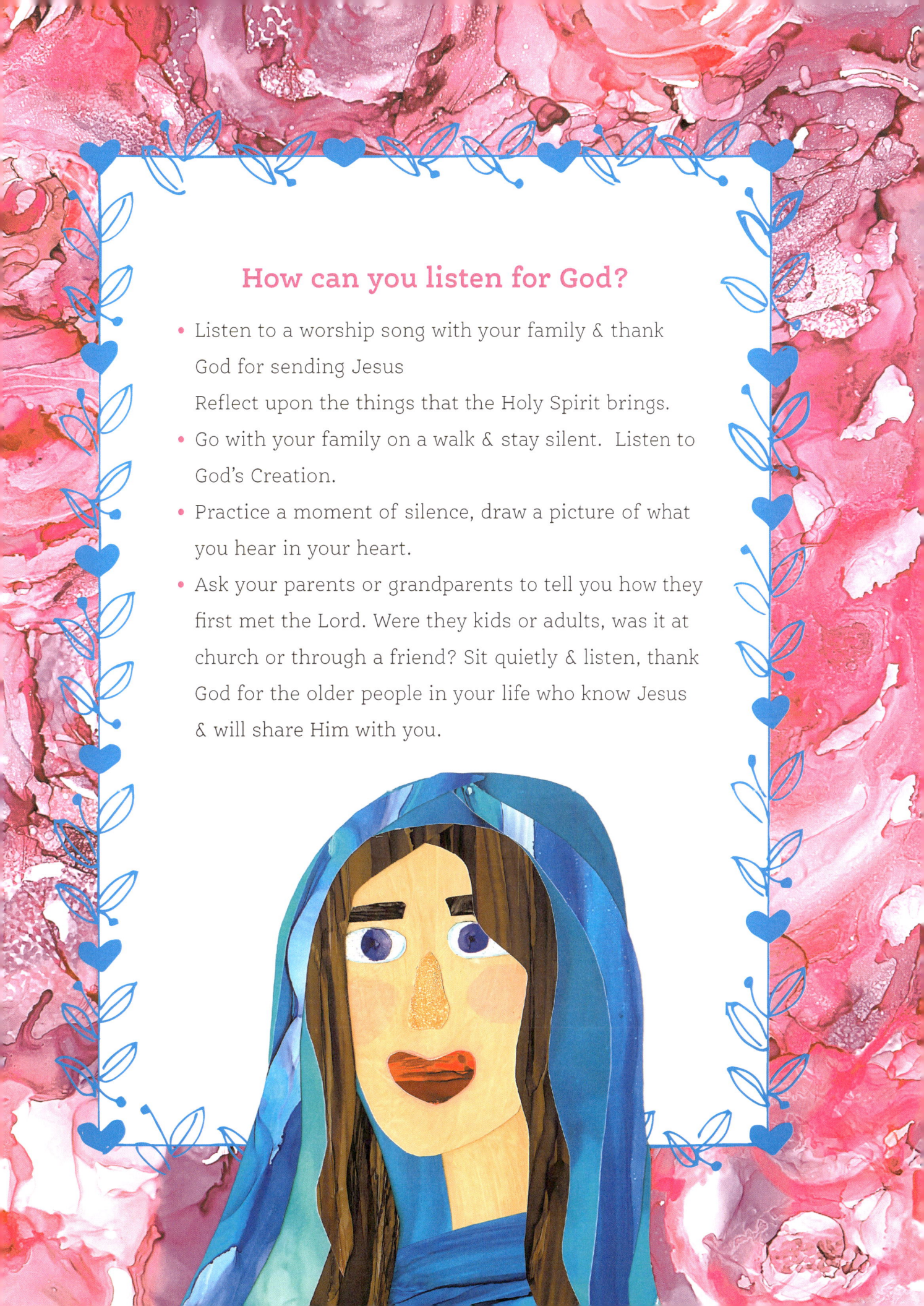

Abide

Like Joseph

**Trust in the Lord with all your heart.
Do not depend on your own understanding.
In all your ways obey Him.
Then He will make your paths smooth and straight.**

Proverbs 3:5-7

Joseph had to trust in God & Abide in Him. Abide means to stay close to God and Joseph needed to do just that! Joseph's plan was going to change. He needed to Abide with God, & trust him to make his path straight. The path Joseph had to take was all the way to Bethlehem & he had to take Mary who was pregnant with Baby Jesus in her belly. When there was no room at the inn, Joseph had to stay close to God and trust that God would provide a safe place for Jesus to be born.

How can you Abide, stay close to Jesus and walk the path that He has for you?

- Choose a place outside or in your home and go there each day this month to pray. Of course you know you can pray any where, any time, but by setting a habit of a place every day, it will help you remember to spend time talking to God.
- Visit someone who is lonely spend time being a friend to them, share that Jesus loves them.
- Choose a family devotional, sit together each morning or evening together and talk about what God is saying through His word to you.
- Have your mom & dad help you write memories of when God helped you or them through a challenging situation. Cut the paper into strips & put them in a jar or basket. Pull one out each day, read it, remember it, & thank God.

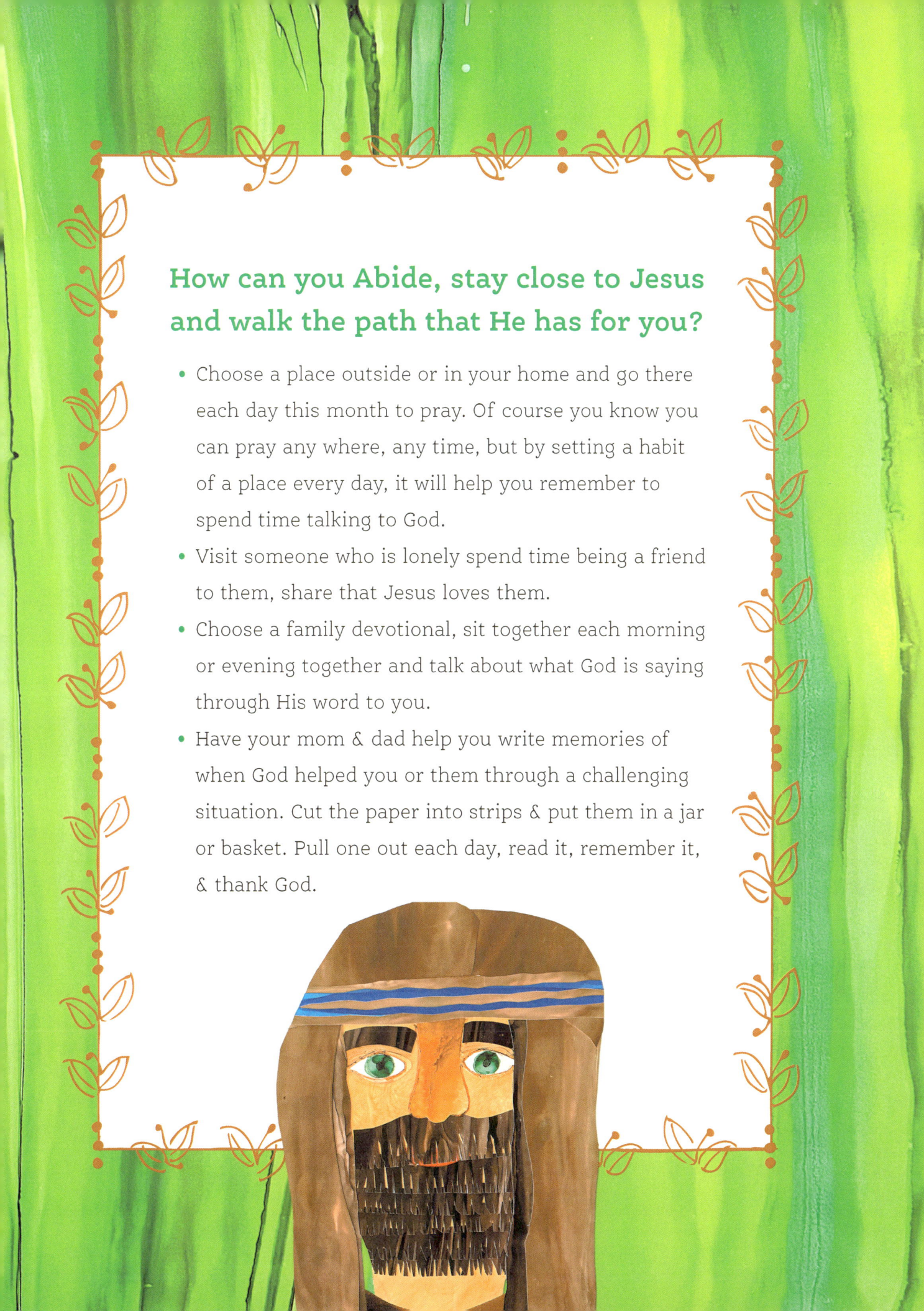

Believe

like the Shepherds

— 🌱 —

Truly, truly, I say to you, whoever hears my word and believes Him who sent me has eternal life. He does not come into judgment, but has passed from death to life.

John 5:24

The Shepherds were out in the fields, a lonely place to be. Suddenly, the Angel arrived sent by God to Proclaim the message, "I bring you good news of great joy for ALL people" What? All people!!! Yes, Jesus came for all of us. He came for the young, the old, the rich, the poor, the brave, the scared, all who will Believe and love Him! That is exactly what the Shepherds did. They ran to Jesus, bowed down, and worshiped Him.

How can you Believe & show others that you Believe in Him?

- Tell your family about the Shepherds. What did they do when the Angels told them about Jesus? What would you do?
- With your mom and dad, pray for a friend who needs to know Jesus
- Draw a picture of the nativity scene and use it to teach someone the nativity story
- As a family, light a candle and pray for children around the world that they may know Jesus.
- With your family, pray and thank God for sending His son to save us!

GiVE
Like the Wise Men

Each of you should give what you have decided in your heart to give. You shouldn't give if you don't want to. You shouldn't give because you are forced to. God loves a cheerful giver.

2 Corinthians 9:7

The Wise Men brought very precious gifts to Baby Jesus. Did Jesus need gifts? Of course not! He is the King of Kings, God's Son, holy and mighty. Yet they brought wonderful, meaningful gifts to honor and worship Him. Gold, Frankincense, and Myrrh honored God's royalty, holiness, and sacrifice. What do the gifts you give say about your love for friends or family. Do gifts have to cost money? What gift would you give to Jesus?

How can you Give to your family, community, and God?

- Ask your family, what gift they would give to Jesus. Draw a picture of those things and hang it so your family can see it all season.
- Make a hand made gift for someone today.
- Give a smile or hug to someone who needs it today.
- Draw a picture of the wisemen and use it to tell the story of the gifts they brought to baby Jesus.
- Choose one of your toys or books and give it to someone who will love it.
- As a family, give to someone in need. Pack a box or bag with food, or clothing to share with someone who has less than you.
- Thank God for all you are blessed with. Make a paper chain with one blessing written on each link. Decorate your Christmas tree, doorway, or mantle with this chain of blessing.

Shine
Like the Star

You are the light of the world. A city set on a hill cannot be hidden. Nor do people light a lamp and put it under a basket, but on a stand, and it gives light to all in the house. In the same way, let your light shine before others, so that they may see your good works and give glory to your Father who is in heaven.

Matthew 5:14-16

The Star of Bethlehem shone brightest of all the stars that night. It had the important job of leading people to find the new Baby King Jesus. All who saw him bowed down to worship. Why do people need to find Jesus today?

How can you Shine to lead friends to find & worship Jesus?

- Draw a picture of the star. Tell your family why God placed it over Baby Jesus
- Tell a friend the true meaning of Christmas, use this book to help share that Jesus is the Light of the World.
- Make a commitment not to argue with your family, especially in public. People will notice and you will shine.
- Memorize Matthew 5:16.
- Names some gifts & talents God has given to you? How can you use those to shine?
- Parents, name 5 ways you saw your kids shine this week. Kids, name 5 ways you saw your parents shine this week. Kids, draw a big star! Write or draw a picture of these shining actions & hang the picture where you can see it to remind you to keep shining every day!
- Choose joy in a difficult situation.
- Pray and ask God to show you how to shine

About the Author & Musician

Jamie and Chris Kearney are the happily married parents of Isabella & Isaiah Kearney and daughter in-law Hannah Kearney. Raising kids, homeschooling, and teaching the love of the Lord was their greatest joy! They have continued celebrating that joy for two decades, teaching at The Village Chapel in Nashville TN, where Jamie serves as the Director of Children's Ministry and Chris serves faithfully beside her each week, musically making every Bible story she shares come to life. In their younger years, Jamie and Chris traveled together in the Contemporary Christian Band, "Bash-N-the Code" followed by years with the Billy Graham Evangelistic Association where Chris played drums for the crusades worship band and together with there kids they led Family Camps at the BGEA Cove Camps.

Through the gift of family, God grows His plan for love and salvation. God chose to send His Son through a family, teaches us to build His family in the church, the Body of Christ, and just like the characters in this story, gives us each a purpose and talent to carry out His mission.

With the release of their first book "Twas the Night of First Christmas" Jamie and Chris hope to creatively share the Good News of Jesus through sight, sound, and with a call to serve the Lord together as a family.

Find more projects like this, at **jamieandchriscreate.com** & on Youtube: **Jamie and Chris Create**

www.ingramcontent.com/pod-product-compliance
Lightning Source LLC
Chambersburg PA
CBRC091211010526
44119CB00020B/371